The Year of the Bible REVISED

An Enhanced Guide to Reading Scripture Together

Participant's Book

The Year of the Bible REVISED
An Enhanced Guide to Reading Scripture Together

James E. Davison

Scripture quotations in this publication are from the New Revised Standard Version (NRSV) of the Bible, copyright © 1989 by the Division of Christian Education of the National Council of Churches of Christ in the U.S.A. Used by permission.

The schedule of readings for *The Year of the Bible* originally appeared in *Daily Devotions: Encounters with God* and *Discovery* and is reprinted by permission from Scripture Union, P.O. Box 6720, Wayne, PA 19087.

Additional copies of this book and other materials for *The Year of the Bible* may be obtained by calling 1-800-524-2612.

Revised edition
Witherspoon Press
Louisville, Kentucky
PRINTED IN THE UNITED STATES OF AMERICA

CONTENTS

Preface to the Revised Edition

I first introduced the idea of *The Year of the Bible* to the staff and members of Westminster Presbyterian Church in Pittsburgh, Pennsylvania. Since that time, I have heard many stories of how reading through the entire Bible—either along with a congregation or individually—has opened people's eyes to the riches of the Scriptures, deepened family and church relationships, or generally strengthened the faith of the persons who have followed the schedule of readings in this book. Some of those stories have been simply amazing, and I am thankful that the program has been so useful to so many people.

Here I simply want to thank, once again, the members of Westminster—especially those who helped me plan and implement the program, first at the church, and later for more than eighty congregations in Pittsburgh Presbytery. I wish to thank, too, the staff in the denominational offices of the Presbyterian Church (U.S.A.) in Louisville, Kentucky. The Congregational Ministries Division first published the program, and now Congregational Ministries Publishing has arranged for a second edition.

And finally, my thanks to all who have participated in the program, who have encouraged each other to keep with it when the readings felt tedious, and who have borne their own testimony to family, to friends—and sometimes to me—about what *The Year of the Bible* was doing in their hearts and lives. It is my fervent hope that readers of this new edition will experience the same joy and growth as they live with the Scriptures this year.

James E. Davison

To the Reader

You are about to start an adventure! Over the next months, as you read the Bible, you will visit a series of foreign cultures, spread across many centuries, with customs and expectations that will seem very different from your own. Some things will sound familiar—for example, "Love your neighbor as yourself"—but many others will seem quite unusual and foreign, such as the ritual and food laws of the early Old Testament. Regardless, as you let yourself settle into this "strange new world," you will find insights and riches in abundance for living in the world you inhabit today.

To assist you as you enter into this "strange new world," I have inserted a new section titled "In the Spotlight" for each month into this edition of *The Year of the Bible* Participant's Book. Some of these articles will highlight customs and cultural practices, while others will offer guidance as you seek to understand and interpret the biblical literature. These articles should make your reading easier, and they may help you grasp the meaning and value of the texts more fully.

Over the years since I first developed *The Year of the Bible,* I have been asked a number of questions by those who were starting out on this adventure. As you begin, let me mention a few of those questions and offer some brief responses. I hope these comments will help ease your way into the readings.

What Version Should I Read?

One of the first questions many people ask about participating in *The Year of the Bible* is what version of the Bible they should read. The first part of the answer: no one version is best for all people! Some translations are literal, trying to provide word-for-word translations as much as possible. In contrast, other translations paraphrase the biblical text loosely, with the intent of bringing the meaning out in contemporary language. Still other translations attempt to find a middle ground.

The New Revised Standard Version (NRSV) is a good example of a more literal translation, while The Message, produced by Pastor Eugene Peterson, is a good example of a paraphrase. The New International Version (NIV) is an example of a version that falls between these two. As you probably know, many other translations are in each of these categories.

Each style of translation has its value. Generally, literal versions are better suited for study, while paraphrases lend themselves to effective devotional reading. The best version for you to use is probably the one that you find most comfortable, such as a Bible that you have had for years. However, it might be the one that you purchase after comparing a few in a local bookstore. Some people who decide to participate in *The Year of the Bible* want to start fresh by reading a new Bible.

If you wish to begin with a new Bible, I encourage you not only to compare versions, but also to consider buying your chosen version in a study Bible format. Study Bibles contain a wealth of information about the background of the passages you are reading and explain terms that may be unfamiliar to you. A study Bible can add to your insight as you make your way through the Old and New Testaments.

How Should I Read?

The primary point of *The Year of the Bible* is simply to get into the Bible—to see the entire panorama of the biblical world and to gain a sense of the whole of God's revelation to us. The one-year period provides a good way to help you accomplish this. For many people, it requires a challenge like this—reading all sixty-six books of the Old and New Testaments in one year—to keep at it.

The downside to this time frame, as you can imagine, is that most people will not have much time to read in depth. It will take approximately twenty minutes to read the daily assignment. To read deeply and to reflect on the meaning of the passages will take considerably longer. If you can take the time only to read the material and to think about it a little, that will be sufficient for this year.

However, if you are able to set aside more time, either daily or occasionally, then I recommend that you take some time to reflect on questions like these:

- What are the primary themes in these passages?
- What do I find here that is new, different, strange, or fascinating?
- What insights do I gain here that I can apply to my own life and faith?

You might jot down your thoughts on these, or similar, questions in a notebook. Many people will attest to the value of keeping a journal of their thoughts, questions, and insights as they read the Bible. Over time, you will discover that your journaling helps strengthen your spiritual life and gives you a deeper sense of God's presence in your life.

What If I Get Behind?

You can probably count on getting behind now and then! You are embarking on a yearlong project with readings for each day of the year. Even with the best of intentions and plans, you are likely to find that "life intervenes." Emergencies, deadlines at work, unexpected visits from relatives, and many other unplanned-for events will likely dot your calendar. At such times, you may have to set your reading aside.

Of course, when you get behind it is best to catch up as soon as possible. If you find that you are two weeks behind—or more!—then I recommend that you pick up your reading with the selections scheduled for the current day. As time permits, begin reading the materials you have skipped. It will not be long before you have caught up.

Now it's time to start reading! The articles in this book are designed to provide an overview of the readings for each month. They will give you some guidance regarding the major things to look for and some pitfalls to avoid. Refer to each month's article occasionally as you do your readings. You will find that the articles help keep you on track, while offering a suggestion now and then that will make your reading more enjoyable.

Finally, let me simply say "thank you." I am grateful for your interest in reading the Bible in this program. I pray that, by the power of God's Spirit, *The Year of the Bible* will have a strong impact on you, and your congregation, too. Throughout the year, may the familiar words of the psalmist prove themselves true for you: "Your word is a lamp to my feet and a light to my path" (119:105).

JANUARY

Here it is! *The Year of the Bible*. This year you will be reading the entire Bible from beginning to end. For many people, this will be the first time doing so. For others, it will not be new at all. Either way, you can expect to make fascinating discoveries and gain a deeper understanding of your faith. As followers of Jesus Christ, we affirm that this book is life-giving; it comes to us as God's very Word. That means you can also expect that God's Spirit will speak to you as you progress through each day's readings.

You will notice that the schedule of readings calls for two chapters of the Old Testament each day. Usually, these are paired with one chapter from the New Testament. Twice weekly, a selection from Psalms replaces the New Testament reading. This design introduces variety into the daily readings. Some sections, particularly in the Old Testament, are lengthy and similar in content. They can seem repetitious if you read them continuously. This schedule avoids that problem and tends to keep your reading fresher and livelier.

This month you will start reading at the beginning of both Testaments. Some of the material will be familiar to you, but other things may seem quite new, even strange at times. In

Day	Scripture Reading
1	Genesis 1, 2/Matthew 1
2	Genesis 3, 4/Matthew 2
3	Genesis 5, 6/Matthew 3
4	Genesis 7, 8/Psalms 1, 2
5	Genesis 9–11/Matthew 4
6	Genesis 12, 13/Matthew 5
7	Genesis 14, 15/Psalms 3, 4
8	Genesis 16, 17/Matthew 6
9	Genesis 18, 19/Matthew 7
10	Genesis 20, 21/Matthew 8
11	Genesis 22, 23/Psalms 5, 6
12	Genesis 24, 25/Matthew 9
13	Genesis 26, 27/Matthew 10
14	Genesis 28, 29/Psalms 7, 8
15	Genesis 30, 31/Matthew 11
16	Genesis 32, 33/Matthew 12
17	Genesis 34–36/Matthew 13
18	Genesis 37, 38/Psalm 9
19	Genesis 39, 40/Matthew 14
20	Genesis 41, 42/Matthew 15
21	Genesis 43, 44/Psalm 10
22	Genesis 45, 46/Matthew 16
23	Genesis 47, 48/Matthew 17
24	Genesis 49, 50/Matthew 18
25	Exodus 1, 2/Psalms 11, 12
26	Exodus 3, 4/Matthew 19
27	Exodus 5, 6/Matthew 20
28	Exodus 7, 8/Psalms 13, 14
29	Exodus 9, 10/Matthew 21
30	Exodus 11, 12/Matthew 22
31	Exodus 13, 14/Matthew 23

the Old Testament, we will be reading mostly from the book of Genesis. Genesis gives us the basic background for the people of Israel. The patriarchs—Abraham, Isaac, Jacob, and Jacob's sons—are the center of the story. However, Abraham does not appear until Genesis 12. The first eleven chapters deal with the prehistory of Israel. They are the stories that place Israel within the context of world history.

As you read, try not to be caught up in discussions of how these events relate to modern science. It is more useful to ask yourself what these stories would have meant to the children of Israel as they heard them told many times. Notice that, even though God creates light immediately, the sun, the moon, and the stars are not created until much later. For our scientific understanding, that sounds strange; however, it is a good way of pointing out that the gods worshiped by neighboring peoples are not gods at all. The nations surrounding Israel believed in many gods. For them, the sun, the moon, and the stars were divine. The implications for the religious beliefs of other nations are clear. There is only one God. This God is above all things, and God has created all things.

Likewise, the story of Adam and Eve in Genesis 2 and 3 shows us what human nature is like. It tries to explain in a simple manner that God has not brought evil into the world. Humans are responsible for perpetuating evil. This and the later stories in this section attempt to show, in a way that is clear to all generations, how God first interacted with human beings, how evil increased rapidly in the world, and how, because of that, God pronounced judgment on human beings.

In Genesis 12, the story moves to the ancestors of Israel, beginning with Abraham. You will discover as you read these stories that the fathers and mothers were not necessarily such wonderful people. For example, Jacob's deceitful behavior is questionable at best. You will see, too, that polygamy was an accepted practice. However, you will also notice that the stories make it clear that polygamy does not work out very well!

All the way through, it is important to note the theme of God's promise and faithfulness to the people God has chosen and their attempts, even though halting, to be faithful to the Lord. God's covenant remains firm even when these people cannot live up to it. The story of Joseph, especially, shows us how God can help a person who is faithful to God. It also explains how the children of Israel end up in Egypt and must be brought back to the Promised Land by Moses at the time of the Exodus.

In the New Testament, we will be reading the Gospel of Matthew. You may know that, while Matthew appears first in the New Testament, it was probably written after Mark. Nearly all scholars believe that

Matthew and Luke used Mark as they wrote their Gospels. All three of these Gospels give a sequential account of Jesus' life. Mark, however, does not pick up the story until Jesus' baptism, while Matthew begins with a genealogy and a story of Jesus' birth. Matthew's striking introduction probably led the early church to think that this Gospel was composed first and thus that it should certainly be placed first in the New Testament. It has been ever since!

Matthew's story about Jesus is straightforward. There are a few themes to keep in mind. A primary theme is that Jesus is the Messiah, the anointed king, for the Jews. This is evident already in the genealogy of Jesus in chapter 1. The family tree is framed in three sets of fourteen generations. Matthew uses this neat and stylized form for the genealogy so that he can emphasize Jesus' descent from David. According to the Jewish manner of counting, the name *David* totaled fourteen. Three sets of fourteen indicate that Jesus is the Davidic son fully, completely, and perfectly.

Another theme to watch for in Matthew is the call to the church to be obedient to God. Watch for references to living a righteous, good life, as in the parable of the sower (ch. 13), in which seed sown on good soil brings forth abundant grain. Or notice the Sermon on the Mount (chs. 5—7), which gives a compelling picture of a serious Christian life. The idea of discipleship is tied to this. Like the original Twelve, Christians are to be disciples of their Master. They are to follow him, serving others without regard to themselves.

Matthew emphasizes that the kingdom of heaven—another theme of the Gospel—is open to those who do the will of God. Nothing else, whether mighty works (7:21–23) or family ties (12:46–50), will get a person into the kingdom. Observe the importance of the kingdom as you read Matthew. To belong to it may well mean persecution and suffering now, but it will also bring ultimate blessedness. To be outside the kingdom, however, will mean final judgment when our resurrected Lord returns in power.

In the Spotlight: January

The Family of Abraham

Later biblical and ecclesiastical history speaks of the patriarchs—Abraham, Isaac, and Jacob—as the fathers of the faith. Similarly, their wives— Sarah, Rebekah, and Leah and Rachel—are often called matriarchs. The implication is that these people serve as ideals for later believers in Israel's God. As you read this month, however, you may wonder how well they actually serve as models of faith for Israel or for us.

The stories of Abraham's family manifest an amazing amount of unsavory behavior. Greed, lying, envy, and doubt: Genesis does not offer a happy history. The patriarchs and matriarchs are a not-so-healthy bunch. In that regard, it is wise to remember that they are not so different from us. We cannot criticize them or snicker at their foibles without implicitly judging our own.

Students of family systems theory will detect in these accounts some examples of the behavior of family members across time. Each of these persons tends to be locked into certain patterns of conduct that pass down through the generations. Notice, for instance, that Jacob (with his mother, Rebekah) deceives his father, Isaac, when he is old and blind. Shortly, Jacob will be deceived in turn by his uncle, Laban, who happens to be Rebekah's sister. Later, Jacob's sons will deceive him. When they provide what appears to be proof that his favorite son, Joseph, has been killed, Jacob spends much of the rest of his life in mourning.

Other tendencies in families are on display here, too. You might think, for example, of parental favoritism. Isaac prefers Esau, while his wife prefers Jacob. Jacob, in turn, favors Joseph, the son of his favored wife, Rachel. The tendency to get support by building interpersonal triangles shows itself, too. As mentioned above, Rebekah connives with Jacob against Isaac. Earlier, Sarah had called on Abraham to exclude Hagar, and later Jacob's sons would gang up on Joseph.

These stories suggest that the family of Abraham endured some rocky relationships from generation to generation. Yet these people served Israel as the fathers and mothers of their faith. In spite of what we might expect, the Bible never idealizes human beings. The heroes of faith are always shown to be fallible, and ultimately that makes the message of the Scriptures all the more realistic and believable.

FEBRUARY

Day	Scripture Reading
1	Exodus 15, 16/Psalms 15, 16
2	Exodus 17, 18/Matthew 24
3	Exodus 19, 20/Matthew 25
4	Exodus 21, 22/Psalm 17
5	Exodus 23, 24/Matthew 26
6	Exodus 25, 26/Matthew 27
7	Exodus 27, 28/Matthew 28
8	Exodus 29, 30/Psalm 18
9	Exodus 31, 32/Acts 1
10	Exodus 33, 34/Acts 2
11	Exodus 35, 36/Psalm 19
12	Exodus 37, 38/Acts 3
13	Exodus 39, 40/Acts 4
14	Leviticus 1–3/Acts 5
15	Leviticus 4, 5/Psalms 20, 21
16	Leviticus 6, 7/ Acts 6
17	Leviticus 8, 9/Acts 7
18	Leviticus 10–12/Psalm 22
19	Leviticus 13, 14/Acts 8
20	Leviticus 15, 16/Acts 9
21	Leviticus 17, 18/Acts 10
22	Leviticus 19, 20/Psalms 23, 24
23	Leviticus 21, 22/Acts 11
24	Leviticus 23, 24/Acts 12
25	Leviticus 25, 26/Psalm 25
26	Leviticus 27/ Numbers 1/Acts 13
27	Numbers 2, 3/Acts 14
28	Numbers 4, 5/Acts 15

We are starting our second month of *The Year of the Bible*. By now, you have probably been able to settle into some sort of routine for your reading. By now, too, you may have fallen behind a few times. You should assume that this will happen occasionally in an undertaking like this! Try not to get too far behind, however, because then it is easy to give up on the entire project.

The Old Testament readings this month are primarily from Exodus and Leviticus. Exodus contains the familiar story of Israel's escape from bondage in Egypt. The first twenty chapters are the most exciting, as they tell us about Moses' life story, the burning bush, the plagues, the parting of the Red Sea, and the giving of the Ten Commandments.

Many people have pointed out that the plagues (as well as the Red Sea and the manna and quail in the wilderness) all have parallels in natural events, so that what is miraculous in them is not so much the extraordinary events themselves, but the timing: they occur as they are predicted by Moses, God's servant. An important element of Exodus is God's giving of the name to Israel in chapter 3. The meaning of the name is mysterious ("I am who I am"), but it obviously indicates God's absoluteness. It is a potent sign that points clearly to the Lord's control over this world.

Once you begin chapter 21, you enter a world of laws and customs, many of which seem strange and alien to us. Some of them will even appear to be unjust or unloving. These kinds of injunctions will be a regular feature of the readings all the way through Deuteronomy. Read them quickly; don't be bogged down. Bear in mind that these laws are given to a group whom God is attempting to turn into a people, and these people live in a world that is in many ways chaotic. As harsh as many of the laws may sound to us, there is a much greater emphasis on justice, equality, and mercy here than there was in the cultures surrounding Israel.

Most of Exodus 25—40 deals with the Tabernacle, the "tent of meeting" that became the center of Israelite worship. With the Holy of Holies as its focal point, the Tabernacle was the place that God promised to be accessible to the people. Here, too, sacrifices could be made to atone for sin and ritual defilement. Exodus closes with an affirmation that God's presence has filled the Tabernacle. The people of Israel can be sure that they belong to and are protected by a gracious and merciful Lord!

Leviticus is a book to read quickly. Much of the material it records, which is intended to regulate religious and civil life for Israel, will be hard to understand and will appear burdensome to us. If you are curious about a regulation or law, a commentary will be helpful. Note in particular chapter 19, with its emphasis on justice and helping the poor. There are certainly implications here for our own attitude toward the less fortunate in our society.

In addition, you may notice the material on atonement in Leviticus 16. This kind of ritual material provides the background for our understanding of Christ's sacrifice on the cross to bring atonement. This is a good example of the point, made by many people, that you cannot really understand the New Testament without grasping the basic concepts of the Old Testament.

Most of our reading from the New Testament this month will be in Acts. This book tells us the story of the growth and development of the earliest church during a period of about thirty years from the time Christ departs in glory. Acts 1:8 sets the outline for the book. It shows an ever-widening circle of testimony to the gospel, until the movement begun in Jerusalem reaches the whole of the world.

Acts points out, too, that the Holy Spirit is God's power in the world that underlies this movement. The Spirit is the motivating force, the impelling energy that transforms a small band of believers into convinced and effective witnesses to the Christ. Look particularly for Luke's references to the Holy Spirit in the life and mission of these early disciples. They are good reminders of our need for the power of God's Spirit to sustain and equip us for our own ministries as Christians.

You will be reading through chapter 15 this month. Most of this half of Acts deals with the original disciples, led by Peter. It is worth reflecting on how different these men are now from the tentative, doubting group of people who were with Jesus only shortly before. Obviously, they have seen the risen Christ and been touched by the Spirit!

Watch for two other things as you read Acts. One is the gradual inclusion, with some hesitations, of non-Jews into the church. The other is the rise of opposition to the new faith. This is tempered at first, but it results eventually in martyrdom for Stephen and James. Contrary to what we hear sometimes these days, witnessing to the gospel does not guarantee a trouble-free existence or a life of ease and comfort!

In the Spotlight: February

Psalms: The Hymns of Israel

A significant part of your readings this year comes from the book of Psalms.

Traditionally, authorship of the psalms has been assigned to King David, who is called the "sweet psalmist of Israel" in 2 Samuel 23:1 (KJV). Although nearly half of the psalms are ascribed to David, scholars differ regarding how many of these he in fact composed. Of the rest, some identify an author, but others list at most only liturgical or musical notations, such as "Selah," "Miktam," or "Maskil."

The meaning of many of these notations is uncertain, but they remind us that the psalms are poetic songs intended for use in worship. Whether composed by an individual in a particular setting—Psalms 51, for example, in connection with David's infidelity with Bathsheba— or written specifically for community use, the psalms came to be associated with worship at the temple, especially in the period after the Babylonian Captivity.

The psalms were written over a period of some six hundred years. Gradually, they were collected into larger and larger units. Eventually, the 150 psalms became five "books" (see the heading of Psalms 1, 42, 73, 90, and 107), which may be a reminder of the five books of Moses. The result is a book that has been called a "collection of collections."

Modern scholars have found that the psalms can be classified into literary types, such as hymns, laments, royal psalms, thanksgiving psalms, and wisdom psalms. While the classifications are not exact, they help us understand the structure of individual psalms. For instance, a *hymn* employs a three-part structure: (a) a joyous call to praise God; (b) reasons for praise; and (c) various expressions of praise. Psalms 19, 47, 65, 115, and 145 are some good examples.

One of the most common forms in Psalms is the *lament,* expressed in the midst of danger or suffering. It consists of (a) a plea for help, (b) an identification of the speaker, (c) expressions of complaints and fears, (d) confessions of trust in God, (e) petitions for help, and (f) assurance that the lament will be heard. Psalms 17, 25, 69, 102, and 142 are some good examples.

Try reading some of the psalms and looking for these structures. Then use them in your own praise and prayer to God. Utilizing these forms may make our own prayers more open, more personal, and more direct. That is undoubtedly why both the Jewish and Christian traditions have always encouraged people of faith to pray the psalms.

MARCH

The Old Testament readings in March come from Numbers and Deuteronomy. Much of the material here will be similar to what you have been reading in the second half of Exodus and Leviticus. Again, don't get bogged down. Read the material quickly, pausing to look more closely at regulations or laws that seem curious or noteworthy. For instance, you may find the material about the "Nazirite vow" in Numbers 6 more interesting if you discover that Samson, the famous strong man of Israel, is a Nazirite (Judges 13).

Numbers, which covers the time of the wilderness wanderings, shows us how far short the Israelites fall when it comes to being righteous and faithful. Notice how many times they complain, commit mutiny, and break the commandments God has so recently given them. Even Aaron and Miriam are jealous of Moses and his position (ch. 12). There is judgment in this book: on foreign nations, on Israel, and even on Moses himself. This is a good reminder to us that God does not simply overlook sin and error; God does not allow the people of Israel (perhaps we should read "Christians" here!) to do as they please and to take the divine call lightly. However, as elsewhere in the Bible, mercy triumphs over judgment: God remains faithful to the covenant with this people.

The name *Deuteronomy*, which means "second Law," indicates that this book is a repetition and summary of the regulations God has given

Israel. It is a kind of constitution for the nation in the Promised Land. The book pictures Israel at the edge of the Promised Land, where Moses in his old age calls upon the people to solemnly reaffirm the covenant. It is difficult to overemphasize the importance of this book. In the New Testament, for instance, Deuteronomy is quoted and alluded to frequently. It has even been said that this book is the spiritual foundation for the modern-day state of Israel.

You may note some special themes in Deuteronomy. A basic one is the emphasis on God's love and Israel's remarkable privilege in enjoying the covenant with the Lord God (4:32–40; 7:6–11). There is also the well-known statement of Israel's faith: "Hear, O Israel: The LORD is our God, the LORD alone" (6:4–9). This passage, called the "Shema," is still the central affirmation of Jewish worship today. Finally, observe the reminder that there are two ways to live life—one good and one evil—along with the appeal to "choose life so that you and your descendants may live" (30:11–20).

In the New Testament this month, we will finish the book of Acts and read much of Romans. Acts centers on Paul and his missionary activities. Many accept the message of this "apostle to the Gentiles," but many others do not. For Jewish listeners, Paul's proclamation is provocative: Gentiles may join the church on an equal footing with Jews. Acceptance of the Jewish Law is not a prerequisite; faith in Christ alone is necessary.

The plot line in Acts moves inexorably toward confrontation with the Jewish authorities in Jerusalem and conflict with the Roman governors. It is interesting to discover that the governors in Palestine are no more concerned with justice than was Pontius Pilate a generation earlier. You will enjoy the last two chapters of Acts especially, where we read about Paul's adventures on his way from Jerusalem to Rome. Try to picture his emotions as he was transported on a small ship on a storm-tossed Mediterranean.

Chapter 28 is the last we hear about Paul's life. Tradition has it that he was released, made his way to Spain to proclaim the gospel there, and eventually returned to Rome. There, we are told, he was imprisoned and later beheaded, the customary mode of execution for Roman citizens.

Romans is Paul's most important letter, not only because of its well-rounded explanation of the gospel, but also because of the influence it has had on so many great leaders of the church at decisive points in Christian history. In the first eight chapters, Paul develops a clear line of argument. Starting with the universal sinfulness of all humanity—both Gentile (1:18–32) and Jew (2:1—3:8)—he concludes that salvation comes by faith alone (chs. 3—5).

Remember, however, that this does not mean that Christians do not need to do good works. It means only that we are not justified because of them. Rather, because we have been justified, we will live a righteous life. You will find a strong and compelling presentation of this in chapters 6—8. Read the last half of chapter 8 a number of times. You will find that it encourages you and gives you reason to rest secure in the midst of the various stresses that we all encounter in contemporary life.

In the Spotlight: March

Torah: God's Instruction to Israel

During these first three months of *The Year of the Bible,* we have been reading the first five books of the Old Testament. In Christian circles, these books are often called the *Pentateuch,* a term that simply derives from the Greek words for "five" and "books." Often, too, they are called "the books of the Law." This, we will see in a moment, is a misleading name.

Both the Jewish and Christian traditions have ascribed these five books to Moses. From the beginning of Exodus, and through Leviticus and Numbers, Moses is the central character around which the story revolves. Now, as we read this month in Deuteronomy, it is Moses who assembles the people to review the commandments as they are about to enter the Promised Land.

You will notice that Deuteronomy repeats many of the laws—including the Ten Commandments—that had been given to Israel earlier. At the same time, the tone of many of the laws and admonitions in Deuteronomy points to a much later time, when Israel had long been established in the land. Scholars generally place the date of the book at or near the time of King Josiah, in the late 600s B.C. In this setting, so different from earlier Israelite life, the book was intended to provide a solid foundation for the religious and communal life of the people.

Much of what we read in these five books can indeed be classified as "law." However, much of it—especially in Genesis and the earlier part of Exodus—is not law at all, but rather stories about the patriarchs and Israel's journey in the wilderness. These stories, naturally, are not told only for their entertainment value. They are intended to give examples to the people about how they should live. In this sense, the intent of the stories is the same as that of the laws: they are meant to *instruct* and to *teach.* Those two words are good translations of the Hebrew word for this material, *Torah.*

When we think of the books of Moses, therefore, it would be best to think of them not as law, but as the "instruction" of Moses. The same is true for later Jewish history. The rabbis and the Pharisees were not fond of Torah simply as a legal code; they revered it because in Torah they encountered God's holy, life-giving teachings and instruction for Israel's well-being.

APRIL

Already we are into the fourth month of the year. If you are on schedule, you have read about a quarter of the Bible. You should find this month's Old Testament readings more appealing than they have been for the last month or two. The reason is that we have finished reading the material on the Law and are now returning to a story line.

The stories in the Old Testament are exciting. They cover the time from the conquest of Canaan, through the period of the judges of Israel, into the time of the first king, Saul. Joshua is the first book we will read. Moses' right-hand man and successor leads the people across the Jordan to finally gain possession of the Promised Land. The unusual events at the fall of Jericho point to the fundamental emphasis of the entire story: God establishes Israel in the land; it is not the people themselves who are conquering Canaan. The conquest is predicated on the assumption that Canaanite culture had reached such a low state, both morally and spiritually, that there was nothing for God to do but to root it out altogether in order to establish a people living according to the Lord's law and will.

As Judges makes clear, Canaanite culture was not overcome in one fell swoop. There was a constant temptation during this period for the people to fall into the patterns and practices of the Canaanites in their midst. A phrase that appears twice in the book describes the chaos and unrighteousness of the times rather well: "All the people did what was right in their own eyes" (17:6; 21:25). Notice that a cyclical pattern emerges as you read the book: Israel is unfaithful to God; God brings judgment upon the people; the people repent; God is merciful and raises up a leader to free them from their enemies; there is peace in the land once more. Then the cycle begins again.

The leaders God raises up are called judges. The two most famous are Gideon and Samson. Since Israel was a patriarchal culture, it is startling to read that one judge is Deborah, a woman. The story of another woman, too, belongs to this period of Judges. The book of Ruth tells of a woman from Moab who adopts Israelite religion when she returns to Bethlehem with her mother-in-law, Naomi. This is a beautiful glimpse of light in a dark period of Israel's history, made more wonderful by the fact that Ruth is a non-Israelite. In a sense, this is an allusion early in the Old Testament to what is proclaimed in the book of Acts: God's grace extends beyond Israel to embrace the Gentiles equally in the covenant people.

First Samuel gives us a look at the time of transition from judges, who arose spontaneously, to kings, who provide dynastic continuity in government. Samuel is a particularly interesting figure. As you read, note that he is a man of many talents—judge, priest, and prophet as well. Samuel anoints Israel's first king, Saul. By the time you finish this month's readings, you will have witnessed Saul, once established as king, fall from grace and enter into rivalry with his eventual successor, David. The backdrop of the story is always the Philistines, a physically larger and more powerful nation. They also possess the ability to make weapons of iron and are a constant military threat to Israel. In the face of Goliath—a visible picture of the Philistines—Israel's only hope is to trust that God will fight on their side. David believes in this hope; Saul does not.

In the New Testament, we will finish the book of Romans this month. Paul is a deep and difficult theologian to read. No matter how often you read his letters, you always have a strong sense that there are depths that you cannot grasp. Nowhere is this more the case than in Romans 9—11, where Paul tries to put into perspective the problem of God's covenant with the Jews and their rejection of Christ. The Gentiles, after all, are now participants in the covenant, too. What, then, of Israel?

As you try to weave your way through these chapters, it may be of some comfort to know that scholars do not agree as to what Paul concludes. The problem is compounded by our knowledge of the multitude of injustices committed against Jews throughout much of

Christian history. Keep in mind one thing: As Paul struggles to deal with the issue, he never weakens his emphasis on the paramount importance of faith in Christ.

When we finish Romans, we will begin reading the Gospel of Mark. You will notice that the material sounds similar to what we read in Matthew. Part of the reason is that Mark was probably the first Gospel to be written and, in all likelihood, Matthew made use of Mark as he wrote his Gospel. Matthew is especially concerned to report in detail what Jesus taught. The Sermon on the Mount is the most obvious example. In contrast, the predominant emphasis in Mark is on what Jesus did.

Mark is an action-packed Gospel, telling us about the amazing and miraculous deeds that Jesus accomplished. Try to breathe in the air of excitement and marvel that Mark felt. You will find this Gospel revitalizing your own sense of awe and wonder as you meet the One to whom the voice from heaven said, "You are my Son, the Beloved; with you I am well pleased" (1:11).

In the Spotlight: April

The Synoptic Gospels

Ever since the early church, people have wondered why we have four Gospels. John is quite different from Matthew, Mark, and Luke, but the latter three seem quite similar. They are called Synoptic (meaning "seen together") Gospels, because they can be set next to each other for easy comparison. All three provide an orderly sequence of Jesus' life and ministry, although Mark begins with Jesus' baptism rather than his birth.

A careful comparison of the Synoptic Gospels has convinced most scholars that Mark was written first. Both Matthew and Luke used Mark's account as the basis for their own. However, Matthew and Luke also contain an abundance of material in common that cannot be found in Mark, most of which is made up of Jesus' sayings. Because of the close similarity in this material, scholars postulate another source used by both Gospels. This is abbreviated as "Q," the first letter in the German word meaning "source" (*Quelle*).

In addition to Mark and Q, Matthew and Luke contain some unique material, most notably in the birth narratives of Jesus. Thus, while the three Synoptic Gospels are very similar in substance, they also provide some quite distinctive material.

Throughout church history, people have tried to harmonize these accounts into one long narrative. On the surface, this seems to be a good idea. After all, such a text allows us to see Jesus' life in a continuous narrative. However, because of minor—and sometimes major—differences in the Gospels, it is difficult to construct a flowing harmony that does not contain contradictions or duplications.

While harmonies of the Gospels continue to be popular, they can deprive us of some of the riches in the individual Gospels. In recent times, therefore, most commentators have found it more illuminating to highlight the distinctive emphases in the Gospels. For example, by comparing how Matthew or Luke differs from Mark, we get a clearer picture of what each wants us to know about Jesus Christ and our relationship to him.

It may be for this reason that God has given us four Gospels. The identity and activity of Jesus is much greater than we can comprehend in one portrait. Each Gospel writer gives us a different perspective and allows us to see additional aspects of this one who—in his life, death, and resurrection—brings amazingly good news to the world.

MAY

May is here. This year that means not only flowers and spring-like weather, but also accounts of the kings of Israel and stories of some of Paul's problems with the church at Corinth.

The Old Testament readings this month begin with 1 Samuel. Chapters 20—31 close out the life and tragic death of Saul. These chapters make for gloomy reading. Saul's fall away from God is coupled with mental instability, to the point that, in desperation, he eventually consults a medium and then commits suicide. The bright spot here is that Saul is unable to poison the strong friendship between his son, Jonathan, and David. David does not appear to have many other friends at this time, and some of the psalms reflect his fear and loneliness.

Second Samuel tells us the story of David's kingship. You will discover that he is a complex person. While David is remembered later as Israel's ideal king, it is obvious that in addition to some exceptionally good qualities, he also has some major character flaws. Note especially how David's own inability to curb his predilection for women results in a household that is anything but harmonious. In many ways, his sons continue the pattern of passion and lack of self-control that marked

Day	Scripture Reading	
1	1 Samuel 20–22/Mark 15	•
2	1 Samuel 23, 24/Mark 16	•
3	1 Samuel 25, 26/Psalm 49	•
4	1 Samuel 27, 28/1 Corinthians 1	•
5	1 Samuel 29–31/1 Corinthians 2	•
6	2 Samuel 1, 2/Psalm 50	•
7	2 Samuel 3–5/1 Corinthians 3	•
8	2 Samuel 6, 7/1 Corinthians 4	•
9	2 Samuel 8–10/1 Corinthians 5	•
10	2 Samuel 11, 12/Psalm 51	•
11	2 Samuel 13, 14/1 Corinthians 6	•
12	2 Samuel 15, 16/1 Corinthians 7	•
13	2 Samuel 17, 18/Psalms 52–54	•
14	2 Samuel 19, 20/1 Corinthians 8	•
15	2 Samuel 21, 22/1 Corinthians 9	•
16	2 Samuel 23, 24/1 Corinthians 10	•
17	1 Kings 1, 2/Psalm 55	•
18	1 Kings 3–5/1 Corinthians 11	•
19	1 Kings 6, 7/1 Corinthians 12	•
20	1 Kings 8, 9/Psalms 56, 57	•
21	1 Kings 10, 11/1 Corinthians 13	•
22	1 Kings 12, 13/1 Corinthians 14	•
23	1 Kings 14, 15/1 Corinthians 15	•
24	1 Kings 16, 17/Psalms 58, 59	•
25	1 Kings 18, 19/1 Corinthians 16	•
26	1 Kings 20, 21/2 Corinthians 1	•
27	1 Kings 22/Psalms 60, 61	•
28	2 Kings 1–3/2 Corinthians 2	•
29	2 Kings 4, 5/2 Corinthians 3	•
30	2 Kings 6, 7/2 Corinthians 4	•
31	2 Kings 8, 9/Psalms 62, 63	•

his life. Nevertheless, you will detect something in David's heart that is good and praiseworthy, a core of faithfulness and trust that is exemplary and draws God's love: he is, after all, a "man after [God's] heart" (1 Samuel 13:14).

As 1 Kings opens, Solomon follows David to the throne. Solomon comes to be known as the model of wisdom in Israel. Chapter 3 gives us two stories that display his discernment in graphic detail. Under Solomon, there is peace and growing prosperity in the land. Major building projects, including a temple to the God of Israel, are instituted. However, over time, Solomon's use of forced labor angers his people, and his enjoyment of royal luxury annoys them. Moreover, Solomon's great wisdom does not prevent him from unwisely leaving a dangerously divided kingdom to his son Rehoboam.

It is not long before the northern tribes break away to establish a kingdom under Jeroboam. Notice that he is from Ephraim, an influential tribe that often rivaled Judah for pride of place among the twelve tribes. This kingdom arrogates to itself the name *Israel*. The remaining tribes in the South come to be known as *Judah*. Since the northern tribes are larger and enjoy a better geographic situation, they quickly come to be much more important in terms of the social-political realities of the day. Their allegiance to the God of Israel, unfortunately, is not very steady. One indication of this is that they set up sanctuaries at Dan and Bethel to keep people from going to Jerusalem. Another is the constant temptation to participate in Baal worship.

"God or Baal" is the real issue in the latter chapters of 1 Kings as we read about the conflicts between Elijah and King AHabakkuk Look carefully at Elijah. He is the prototype of the prophet in Israel. Thus, when we are told of the Transfiguration in the Gospels, Moses and Elijah appear to Jesus. Moses represents the Law; Elijah, the prophets. To understand the problem with Ahab and Jezebel, it is important to realize that their intention was not to deny Israel's God, Yahweh. Rather, they wanted to worship both God and Baal. They wanted to have a portfolio of gods on their side to cover any possible eventualities.

This is a typically polytheistic approach to religion, and it is perfectly understandable to many millions of people, but it is at the same time diametrically opposed to Israel's faith: "If the LORD is God, follow him; but if Baal, then follow him" (18:21). This is the challenge of Elijah on Mount Carmel, and it is crucial to the basic message preached later by all the prophets—and the apostles of Christ as well. Before leaving this story, ask yourself what false gods are in our own generation and whether we, too, need to listen to Elijah.

Most of our New Testament readings this month will be in 1 Corinthians. The Corinthian Christians had great potential, but they had many problems, too. You will notice a tone of distress, and sometimes anguish, in Paul's writing. (This distress is even stronger in 2 Corinthians.) An underlying difficulty was pride. Divisions were deep and sharp, and scandals sometimes rocked the church. It is refreshing to realize that some beautiful passages in the letter are composed as Paul is trying to bring relief to a not-so-pleasant situation. You may think of his description of the words of institution for the Lord's Supper in chapter 11, or the wonderful hymn on love in chapter 13.

There is not enough space here to deal in depth with the comment that Paul makes about women being "silent in the churches" (14:34), but you will certainly notice it! This appears to be a comment for the messy Corinthian situation, rather than a command for all congregations at all times. In fact, even in Corinth, there are times when Paul approves of women speaking publicly—even in an authoritative role (11:2–16).

Finally, 1 Corinthians contains a compelling witness to the hope and assurance that Christ's resurrection offers. If you are wondering about your faith, if you feel a questioning tug within you about whether faith in God really makes sense, read chapter 15 again. There Paul reminds us that God speaks the last word in this mysterious and sometimes disastrous world. "Thanks be to God, who gives us the victory through our Lord Jesus Christ" (v. 57).

In the Spotlight: May

The Gospel at Corinth

Each of Paul's main letters addresses a small Christian community living in a predominantly Gentile environment in the Roman Empire. Paul writes primarily to encourage and exhort his recipients to faithfulness despite the temptations they faced living in societies with such divergent worldviews. To understand the letters, it helps to learn a little about the cultures and values of the cities to which the letters were written.

Corinth is one of the more interesting of these cities. It sat astride the only land route between the Peloponnese in the south and the rest of Greece to the north. A harbor gave access eastward to the Aegean, while a lengthy channel ran westward to the Adriatic. Boats regularly traversed this channel, even though it required hauling cargo across a narrow isthmus. So valuable was the route that some ancient rulers, including Nero, attempted to cut a canal through the rock, an achievement that succeeded only in the late nineteenth century.

Corinth was a relatively "new" city. An earlier settlement had been destroyed in 146 B.C. Founded anew by Julius Caesar one hundred years later, the town grew quickly. Opportunities for trade led to a flood of new wealth and sharp class distinctions. A highly competitive spirit accompanied all this economic activity, as did lax moral standards. The influx of people to this prosperous city also brought a wide range of cultural and religious practices, which were oftentimes exotic.

Easily overlooked in this active urban environment was the little church to which Paul addressed at least two letters. The members came mostly from the lower classes, although there were also some wealthy members. Likely, "the church" was composed of a few house churches, where small groups of people gathered to worship. The social divisions in the city were equally noticeable in the church. Evidence of them shows up in such things as the dispute over sharing the Lord's Supper (1 Corinthians 11), the rivalry regarding baptism (1 Corinthians 1), or the questions about Paul's qualifications as an apostle (2 Corinthians 10–13).

That Paul's relationship with these believers was difficult is readily apparent from his letters. Probably to counteract their competitive attitudes, Paul stresses, early in 1 Corinthians, that the gospel allows no room for pride. To underscore this, he says, he proclaims "Christ crucified" (1:23). Paul hopes to foster a similar mind-set among the members of this small, divisive community that has come to believe in the gospel of Jesus Christ.

JUNE

When we have finished the readings for June, we will be halfway through *The Year of the Bible*. This is a good time to look back over the readings we have completed thus far, to give thanks for this accomplishment, and to ask for help in continuing until the end of the year. The discipline of regular reading, no doubt, has been profitable, so that you have found it to be not only a rigorous challenge but also a valuable time that enriches your faith and draws you closer to Christ Jesus.

The Old Testament material this month covers the second half of 2 Kings and the books of the Chronicles. As you read 2 Kings, remember that the people are no longer united; there are two kingdoms—Israel in the North and Judah in the South. At times the kingdoms work together, but there is no love lost between them. Israel, in particular, gives us a dismal picture of idolatry, Canaanite worship (the people seem to have missed Elijah's message about choosing God or Baal!), and social injustice. Before long, Israel becomes entangled in an unholy alliance with the Assyrians, the rising power in the East. When Israel later attempts to revolt, the kingdom is destroyed.

Day	Scripture Reading
1	2 Kings 10–12/2 Corinthians 5
2	2 Kings 13, 14/2 Corinthians 6
3	2 Kings 15, 16/Psalms 64, 65
4	2 Kings 17, 18/2 Corinthians 7
5	2 Kings 19, 20/2 Corinthians 8
6	2 Kings 21, 22/2 Corinthians 9
7	2 Kings 23–25/Psalms 66, 67
8	1 Chronicles 1–3/2 Corinthians 10
9	1 Chronicles 4–6/2 Corinthians 11
10	1 Chronicles 7–10/Psalm 68
11	1 Chronicles 11–14/2 Corinthians 12
12	1 Chronicles 15, 16/2 Corinthians 13
13	1 Chronicles 17, 18/Galatians 1
14	1 Chronicles 19–21/Psalm 69
15	1 Chronicles 22, 23/Galatians 2
16	1 Chronicles 24–27/Galatians 3
17	1 Chronicles 28, 29/Psalms 70, 71
18	2 Chronicles 1, 2/Galatians 4
19	2 Chronicles 3–5/Galatians 5
20	2 Chronicles 6, 7/Galatians 6
21	2 Chronicles 8, 9/Psalm 72
22	2 Chronicles 10–12/Ephesians 1
23	2 Chronicles 13–15/Ephesians 2
24	2 Chronicles 16, 17/Psalm 73
25	2 Chronicles 18–20/Ephesians 3
26	2 Chronicles 21–23/Ephesians 4
27	2 Chronicles 24–25/Ephesians 5
28	2 Chronicles 26–28/Psalm 74
29	2 Chronicles 29, 30/Ephesians 6
30	2 Chronicles 31, 32/Luke 1:1–38

An especially significant consequence of this is that, as part of their policy of subjugation, the Assyrians deport Israel's leading citizens and resettle foreigners from other parts of the empire in Israel. Israel, now a province of the Assyrian Empire, is named Samaria, after its leading city.

Intermarriages soon occur and the population becomes mixed. This is the origin of the "Samaritans," people who were despised by the Jews in New Testament times. Although the Samaritans continue to worship God and retain a form of the Law of Moses, their adherence to differing traditions and their racially mixed blood make them outcasts in the eyes of Jews in Christ's day.

The situation in Judah to the South is somewhat better, but barely. The line of David continues without interruption, and there are a number of good kings, such as Hezekiah and Josiah. Ahaz and Manasseh, however, are evil—so evil, in fact, that each of them burns a son as an offering to the gods. In other words, they participate in the most depraved practices to which Canaanite religion could descend. You will probably find the account of Hezekiah and Isaiah (2 Kings 18—20) to be the most uplifting part of these stories.

Eventually, Judah's involvement in power politics gets it into trouble with the Babylonians, who are now the major power in the East. Second Kings ends with the story of the destruction of Jerusalem and the end of the kingdom of Judah. By the way, at this point the Ark of the Covenant disappears from the pages of history, never to be seen again.

You will want to read the Chronicles quickly. As you read this material, note that the writer presents David and Solomon as ideal figures by which to gauge later rulers. At the same time, there is a stress on the priesthood, the temple in Jerusalem, and the need to obey the Law of Moses. Looking for these themes will give you a thread to follow as you read.

The New Testament readings for June begin with the last two-thirds of 2 Corinthians. The tone of the letter indicates that Paul has difficulties with this church. In chapters 4 and 5, Paul says that his troubles are ways in which he comes closer to Jesus Christ, and that he looks forward to the time when this present life will give way to the full, eternal life that awaits us in Christ. Read these two chapters several times; let them penetrate your mind and spirit. They can be especially helpful in your own times of trouble.

Chapters 8 and 9 are worth noting as an example of Paul's attitude toward financial resources. When you run into one of those people who comments that "the church is always asking for money," suggest that they read these two chapters! Paul's own sufferings for the gospel come through clearly in the latter part of this letter. Chapter 11, specifically, contains a compelling autobiographical portrait of his life.

We will also be reading Galatians and Ephesians this month. Galatians gives us a sustained discussion of the famous doctrine of the Reformation, "justification by faith alone." How urgent this was for Paul is apparent when you see that he opposed Peter publicly at Antioch (2:11). You will have trouble understanding Paul's reasoning unless you bear in mind that, for Jews, the Law was assumed inviolable and eternal. Paul had believed this once, too, but in light of Christ, he has come to see that the Law is only temporary. A case in point is the prohibition against Jews eating with Gentiles: "for all of you are one in Christ Jesus" (3:28). A useful exercise is to ask ourselves whether there are any areas in our lives where "justification by faith alone" may require us to revise some of our attitudes or actions.

Ephesians, since it does not address acute difficulties and problems, is much more serene in tone than Galatians. It, too, talks about justification and, like the end of Galatians, offers comments on living as Christians in the world. In fact, Ephesians contains some practical advice about this. Even more significant, perhaps, are the appealing statements about the riches of God in Jesus Christ. Notice how frequently this theme returns in the first four chapters. The benediction at the end of chapter 3 is worth pondering: We believe in a God who is able to accomplish in us "far more than all we can ask or imagine" (v. 20). Isn't that a good verse to remember when you fall behind in your readings for *The Year of the Bible?*

In the Spotlight: June

Israel's Rulers

Until the time of the prophet Samuel, the tribes of Israel had lived in a loose confederation, with leadership arising as needed in the form of judges. Surrounded by other, more urban areas where kings ruled, the Israelites occasionally expressed a desire for the same sort of political structure. However, as the judge Gideon affirmed when he was offered the kingship, Israel's traditional principle was that "the LORD will rule over you" (Judges 8:23).

For a time, this ideal of theocratic rule acted as a brake on the development of kingship in Israel. With the election of Saul, however, Israel set out on a new political path. His failures serve as an early reminder of how quickly the monarchy could become remote from the common people. Much later, the Torah will include injunctions against royal power and pride (Deuteronomy 17:14–20).

Saul's downfall brings to the throne David, a much more popular and successful monarch. Under David and Solomon, the kingdom grew in power and prestige. However, following their reigns, the northern tribes seceded. For the next two hundred years, there were two parallel kingships in the north and south. Following the destruction of the Northern Kingdom by the Assyrians, the Southern Kingdom survived for another 135 years under the descendents of David, until the fall of Jerusalem to the Babylonians.

In keeping with the earlier hesitations about monarchy, the books of Samuel and Kings point out in detail the spotty record of most of the rulers. Even the ideal king, David, is portrayed with deeply engrained flaws. With later kings, judgment of their reigns is often wholly negative. This attitude contrasts strikingly with other royal records in the ancient Near East. Elsewhere, chronicles of the kings center invariably on the successes of the monarchy while overlooking the failures.

It is noteworthy that the two books of Chronicles, written later in Israel's history, offer something of a parallel to the usual idealizing we see elsewhere. David and Solomon are indeed presented as ideal figures, and Chronicles passes over their flaws. Later kings get no such "pass," of course.

Thus, the earlier ambivalence to monarchy seems to have continued in muted fashion throughout the whole of Israel's history. Chronicles resolves the tension to some degree by presenting the ideal king, David, as an advocate for national worship centered in the temple. Following the destruction of Jerusalem, which effectively ended the kingship, the temple continues to provide a focus for Israel's unity.

JULY

Day	Scripture Reading	
1	2 Chronicles 33, 34/Psalms 75, 76	*
2	2 Chronicles 35, 36/Luke 1:39–80	*
3	Ezra 1, 2/Luke 2	*
4	Ezra 3, 4/Luke 3	*
5	Ezra 5, 6/Psalm 77	*
6	Ezra 7, 8/Luke 4	*
7	Ezra 9, 10/Luke 5	*
8	Nehemiah 1, 2/Psalm 78:1–37	*
9	Nehemiah 3, 4/Luke 6	*
10	Nehemiah 5, 6/Luke 7	*
11	Nehemiah 7, 8/Luke 8	*
12	Nehemiah 9, 10/Psalm 78:38–72	*
13	Nehemiah 11, 12/Luke 9	*
14	Nehemiah 13/Luke 10	*
15	Esther 1–3/Psalm 79	*
16	Esther 4, 5/Luke 11	*
17	Esther 6, 7/Luke 12	*
18	Esther 8–10/Luke 13	*
19	Job 1, 2/Psalm 80	*
20	Job 3, 4/Luke 14	*
21	Job 5, 6/Luke 15	*
22	Job 7, 8/Psalms 81, 82	*
23	Job 9, 10/Luke 16	*
24	Job 11, 12/Luke 17	*
25	Job 13, 14/Luke 18	*
26	Job 15–17/Psalms 83, 84	*
27	Job 18, 19/Luke 19	*
28	Job 20, 21/Luke 20	*
29	Job 22, 23/Psalm 85	*
30	Job 24–26/Luke 21	*
31	Job 27, 28/Luke 22	*

The second half of *The Year of the Bible* begins with some interesting material. In the Old Testament, we start with Ezra, Nehemiah, and Esther. These books record events that occurred during the time following the Babylonian Captivity.

Remember that, when Jerusalem was destroyed and the Jews were carried off to Babylon in 586 B.C., it seemed as if the Jewish nation would cease to exist. However, prophets like Jeremiah promised that God would restore the nation, even after such a great calamity. These seemingly improbable promises were fulfilled when Cyrus, who made Persia the ruling power in the East, allowed the displaced peoples to return to their homelands (Ezra 1; 6).

Ezra records the trek back to Jerusalem around 537 B.C. They built homes and once again made sacrifices to the Lord. Over a twenty-year period, they succeeded in rebuilding the temple. In the next century, Ezra himself went to Jerusalem to help reestablish the Law of Moses in the land. Shortly afterward, Nehemiah went to supervise the rebuilding of the city walls. Note the discouragement in both books: troublesome neighbors, halfhearted allegiance to God, and harsh economic conditions all conspired to make life difficult.

Esther contains the first record of an attempt to destroy a group of Jews who are a minority within another culture. The heroine is not only beautiful, but also upright and good, and there is a delicious irony in the way the "bad guy" of the story, Haman, gets his just deserts. Note that, in later Jewish culture, the primary purpose of the book was to describe the beginnings of the Jewish festival of Purim.

The latter part of July will take us through most of Job. Its main theme is the problem of suffering: "How can bad things happen to good people?" The book reads somewhat like a play. The first two chapters tell the story of a righteous man, Job, who undergoes a succession of disastrous events. The bulk of the book is a series of speeches and responses. Three "friends," who come to offer Job advice and admonition, make the speeches. Unfortunately, they fail miserably as counselors because they never really listen to Job. Their underlying assumption is that Job's great suffering is a clear indication that he is guilty of some major sin. Job responds to their accusations with increasing anger and frustration, claiming all the while that he is innocent.

Since this material is written in a poetic style, you may find the language and imagery somewhat hard to follow, though it is well known in the ancient Near East. Skim through the book quickly, looking for main themes and memorable verses (for example, 4:17; 5:7; 14:1; 14:14; 19:25; 21:17).

We know what Job's friends do not know, namely, that Job has done nothing to deserve his sufferings. That is precisely the point: There is no exact correlation between human sin and suffering on earth. This is what the book was written to show, and it does so effectively. At the end of the book (chs. 38—42), God speaks from the whirlwind, justifying Job's innocence and calling on humans to recognize the mysteriousness of God's ways and the limitations of human knowledge.

The notion that suffering and sin can be equated is an idea that dies hard. In Luke 13, which we also read this month, Jesus deals with the same question. He denies that some Galileans killed by Pilate—and some people killed in Jerusalem when a tower fell on them—were being punished for their sins (vv. 1–5). Many people still feel that those who suffer various scourges such as famine, plagues, or disease are being punished for their sins. When you're tempted to think this way, recall Jesus' succinct reply: "Don't look at others; look to yourself!"

In the New Testament, we will read most of Luke this month. Why do we have more than one Gospel? Primarily, it is because the different writers had different things they wished to emphasize about Jesus. Luke, for instance, delights in stressing the universal scope of the gospel: It is intended for both Jews and Gentiles; it is for the whole world. A telltale sign of this interest is Luke's frequent use of the word *all*. Notice, too, the times when Luke includes Old Testament references to outsiders who were more faithful than the Israelites, such as the widow at Sidon and Naaman the Syrian (4:25–30) or the queen of Sheba and the people of Nineveh (11:29–32).

There are some other special concerns to watch for in Luke. First, there is Luke's interest in the poor. In an affluent society like ours, we are susceptible to the enticing allure of material goods. Luke's stress on the poor reminds us to be thankful for our blessings. More important, it challenges us to practice the same kind of compassion for the needy that Jesus did.

Second, there is an emphasis on the Holy Spirit. You may already have noticed that theme when you read Acts, where Luke underlines the power of the Spirit in the life of the early church. Here in the Gospel of Luke, watch for the times when he speaks about the action of the Spirit in Jesus' own life.

Third, there is the prayer life of Jesus. Observe how often Luke records the fact that Jesus spent time in prayer. Somehow, it seems surprising that Jesus, who had so much to do, took time out for prayer. Maybe it will help us with our own attempts to juggle all the demands in our hectic lives to remember that, if anything, Jesus' busy schedule led him to pray more, not less.

In the Spotlight: July

Queen Esther

The book of Esther is something of an enigma. Two thousand years ago, the rabbis had grave misgivings about including it among the canonical books of the Hebrew Bible. The primary reason is that nowhere in Esther does the name *God* appear. This certainly seems odd for a book of the Bible. At the same time, Esther has always been well loved by the Jewish people, because it relates the story of the origins of Purim, the annual spring feast that celebrates the deliverance of the people of Israel from persecution in the Persian Empire.

Another reason that Esther is revered so greatly is that the book depicts well what the Jews have undergone in so many times and places. Indeed, the book embodies themes that have often plagued human life throughout history: the unjust abuse of minority groups, righteousness prevailing against all odds, the wicked caught in their own traps, and individual courage in the face of persecution.

The plot revolves around an impulsive Persian king, probably to be identified with Xerxes, whose lack of attentiveness allows an evil adviser, Haman, to instigate a persecution of all Jews in the realm. The Jews are saved because the king, in another impulsive act, deposes his upright and beautiful queen, Vashti. Her replacement is the demure and beautiful Esther. Guided by her older cousin, Mordecai, Esther exposes the scheming Haman, who ends up hung from the very gallows he had previously built for Mordecai. The book ends as the feast of Purim is instituted and the Jews enjoy peace and respect throughout the empire.

The book of Esther is enigmatic for another reason. Queen Esther is clearly the hero of the story, but the most heroic figure in the book is Mordecai. He is a good man in many senses of the word. The writer emphasizes his responsibility, uprightness, competence, and loyalty. Mordecai recognizes the danger that Haman's scheming presents to all Jews, including Esther.

Until Mordecai counsels Esther to act, she seems somewhat passive and unaware of her peril. Yet when she hears his words, "Perhaps you have come to royal dignity for just such a time as this" (4:14), she gathers the courage to risk her own position by appealing to the king for justice. Thus, it is that Esther has come to be honored ever since with a book bearing her name.

AUGUST

This month, much of our reading in the Old Testament will be in Proverbs. Proverbs is a part of the biblical material that is called "Wisdom Literature," because it arises from a particular subculture of wise scribes in Israel. Job and Ecclesiastes are two more books in the wisdom tradition.

You will notice immediately that there is a kind of singsong quality to Proverbs. This is due to Hebrew literary style, which often tends to operate by means of poetic repetition or parallelism. The basic unit of thought is a combination of two lines. The first line is a brief statement, while the second line repeats the same idea in different words. For example, notice the statement in 2:6: "For the LORD gives wisdom." The next line repeats this thought: "from [God's] mouth come knowledge and understanding." Oftentimes, the second line will express the opposite idea of the first. Can you find an example? From this basic parallel structure, more complex units are developed. You can see this already in the first six verses of the book.

The helpful aspect of this literary style is that it paints a rich portrait of the topic or theme of the writing. At the same time, however, the singsong style can put a person to sleep! To stay awake, keep your eye on the main theme. Restate that theme in your own words and try to apply it to your own situation. Then you will find that Proverbs can be a powerful, useful book as you attempt to "trust in the LORD with all your heart" (3:5).

Day	Scripture Reading
1	Job 29, 30/Luke 23
2	Job 31, 32/Psalms 86, 87
3	Job 33, 34/Luke 24
4	Job 35, 36/Philippians 1
5	Job 37, 38/Psalm 88
6	Job 39, 40/Philippians 2
7	Job 41, 42/Philippians 3
8	Proverbs 1, 2/Philippians 4
9	Proverbs 3, 4/Psalm 89
10	Proverbs 5, 6/Colossians 1
11	Proverbs 7, 8/Colossians 2
12	Proverbs 9, 10/Psalm 90
13	Proverbs 11, 12/Colossians 3
14	Proverbs 13, 14/Colossians 4
15	Proverbs 15, 16/1 Thessalonians 1
16	Proverbs 17, 18/Psalm 91
17	Proverbs 19, 20/1 Thessalonians 2
18	Proverbs 21, 22/1 Thessalonians 3
19	Proverbs 23, 24/Psalms 92, 93
20	Proverbs 25, 26/1 Thessalonians 4
21	Proverbs 27, 28/1 Thessalonians 5
22	Proverbs 29, 30/2 Thessalonians 1
23	Proverbs 31/Psalm 94
24	Ecclesiastes 1–3/2 Thessalonians 2
25	Ecclesiastes 4, 5/2 Thessalonians 3
26	Ecclesiastes 6, 7/Psalms 95, 96
27	Ecclesiastes 8, 9/1 Timothy 1
28	Ecclesiastes 10, 11/1 Timothy 2
29	Ecclesiastes 12/1 Timothy 3
30	Song of Solomon 1, 2/Psalms 97, 98
31	Song of Solomon 3, 4/1 Timothy 4

Proverbs emphasizes especially the need to gain wisdom. Wisdom is a gift from God. At the same time, it is something that we need to develop and cultivate. If you've been struggling to keep up with the readings for *The Year of the Bible* program, ponder what Proverbs says about the way to acquire this divine wisdom. Wisdom comes from God's law, or the commandments. Translated into our language, this means that wisdom comes from the Bible. We hope that one of the effects of *The Year of the Bible* will be to help us increase in wisdom.

One further thing: Wisdom is important, according to Proverbs, because it provides counsel about the practical question of how we live our daily lives. Do we live wisely or foolishly? All of the suggestions in Proverbs are intended to help us gain the insight we need to live in the former rather than the latter way. This may remind you of Jesus' parable in the Sermon on the Mount. He compares the wise man, who built a house on the rock, to the foolish man, who built on sand. What's the difference between the two? The wise man, says Jesus, builds his life on the words of Jesus (Matthew 7:24–27).

From the cheery optimism of Proverbs, we turn to Ecclesiastes. This is another writing of Wisdom Literature, but here doom and gloom rule. There is quite a diversity of opinion about this book, particularly regarding the identity and viewpoint of the author. Is the writer as pessimistic as he sounds, or is he portraying the depression of a life lived without God? If you are interested in this debate, you can find responses to these questions in the introductions to commentaries on Ecclesiastes. At this point, the author appears to be a sage who chooses Solomon— the prototypical man of wisdom for Israel—as his mouthpiece. He seems to have a pessimistic spirit. He finds the world tragic and, perhaps, meaningless, and he borders on disbelief.

After reading the morning newspaper, you may find his observations about the world right on target: "Vanity of vanities! All is vanity" (1:2). The sage, or "Teacher," points out that the world never seems to get anywhere. Justice is lacking, human toil does not bring relief from the rat race, and death appears to reduce all to the same level. At times, it seems to this writer that it is more blessed to be dead than alive (3:2). Ecclesiastes can be of great service to you if you sometimes struggle with doubt about faith. It may be comforting to know that God does not simply reject people who have difficulty believing. Why, even the author of one of the books of the Bible had serious misgivings about faith in a world like ours!

In the New Testament this month, we will be reading some of the epistles of Paul. As you read, remember that these are real letters written to specific persons and groups. They are not carefully crafted pieces of work intended for a general audience. Have you ever wondered what Paul would have thought had he realized that his epistles would be read by millions of people twenty-one centuries later? How might it have affected what he said and how he said it?

Philippians is a particularly delightful letter. Writing from prison, Paul converses with a congregation that cherished a deep affection for him, and he for them. The theme of joy in the face of adversity runs through the whole letter. We can learn a lot about patience and humility here, too.

First and Second Thessalonians are probably Paul's earliest epistles. Notice the emphasis on Christ's return in glory. It appears that Paul originally thought that Christ would soon return and that the new heaven and new earth would be inaugurated shortly. These letters reflect that viewpoint, as does 1 Corinthians. It is especially interesting to note that Paul has to summon the church at Thessalonica to trust in the fact that Christ Jesus will indeed return in glory. However, he does this so successfully in the first letter that, in the second, he has to caution the people not to carry this to extremes! At the close of the second letter, Paul pronounces a blessing that is worth remembering: "Now may the Lord of peace himself give you peace at all times in all ways. The Lord be with all of you" (3:16).

In the Spotlight: August

The Wise Men of Israel

Wisdom literature comes from "sages," a name given to those in the ancient Middle East who taught wise ways of living. Sages were regularly included in ancient royal courts, where they served as teachers and counselors. They also maintained international contacts and shared their insights from one country to the next. Israel's own sages participated in this movement, exchanging their wisdom and insights with their neighbors.

Much of the Wisdom tradition operates around the so-called "two ways" doctrine, stated classically in Deuteronomy 30:15–20. Depending on which of the two ways a person follows, he or she can expect to be blessed or cursed. The scheme is straightforward: Live a good life, following the Lord, and you can expect comfort and protection in this life. Live in the opposite manner, and you can expect the opposite results. The book of Proverbs is the best example of this philosophy of life, with its uncomplicated aphorisms and imagery.

A careful look at the world shows, unfortunately, that this two-ways scheme does not stand up to the realities of life; our own experience frequently contradicts the doctrine. Nevertheless, this is an appealing idea and it dies hard. From time to time, we are likely to find it appearing subtly in our own attitudes.

The book of Job is written to argue against this view. By this point in Israel's history, the sages have begun to realize that earlier, easier assumptions about God, the world, and human life are more complex than tradition taught. Job is an elaborate story, perhaps based on an ancient account of a righteous person who suffered grievously. It examines—and ultimately rejects—the assumptions of the two-ways doctrine, concluding that the right approach to life is simply to (1) praise God, recognizing the power and mystery of the Lord of the universe, and (2) live like Job, remaining righteous regardless of circumstances.

The kind of skepticism that is budding in Job will come back in Ecclesiastes in full bloom. The author of that book is not certain that life has any meaning at all. Faced with the gloom in the book, we may prefer the happy optimism of the earlier viewpoint!

Still, we should remember that, even though Proverbs presents a philosophy that is too simple, there is something to say for it. Its many sayings contain obvious truths about life, and they are well worth taking to heart.

SEPTEMBER

We are entering the homestretch in our readings. Two-thirds of the readings are behind us, and only one-third remain. At the end of the year, we ought to have a big party to celebrate!

Most of our reading in the Old Testament during September will be in Isaiah. You can gauge the importance of this book from the fact that it is referred to so often in the New Testament. Isaiah has a wonderful feeling for the way God's mercy and justice intermingle. His awareness of God as the "Holy One of Israel" (1:4) is exceptional as well. Notice chapter 6, where his call to be a prophet develops the theme of the holiness of God.

As you will discover in Isaiah, there is a major difficulty in reading the books of the prophets. The prophecies are not written in careful historical order, and often there is no clear reference to the specific situation. This means that, oftentimes, the prophets can be bewildering books to read. Therefore, you will want to read Isaiah quickly, looking for main themes and topics. Search for compelling verses and memorable phrases—ones that sound familiar to you or ones that convey something significant about God's ways with

Day	Scripture Reading
1	Song of Solomon 5, 6/1 Timothy 5
2	Song of Solomon 7, 8/Psalms 99–101
3	Isaiah 1, 2/1 Timothy 6
4	Isaiah 3–5/2 Timothy 1
5	Isaiah 6, 7/2 Timothy 2
6	Isaiah 8, 9/Psalm 102
7	Isaiah 10–12/2 Timothy 3
8	Isaiah 13, 14/2 Timothy 4
9	Isaiah 15, 16/Psalm 103
10	Isaiah 17–20/Titus 1
11	Isaiah 21, 22/Titus 2
12	Isaiah 23, 24/Titus 3
13	Isaiah 25, 26/Psalm 104
14	Isaiah 27, 28/Philemon
15	Isaiah 29, 30/Hebrews 1
16	Isaiah 31, 32/Psalm 105
17	Isaiah 33, 34/Hebrews 2
18	Isaiah 35, 36/Hebrews 3
19	Isaiah 37, 38/Hebrews 4
20	Isaiah 39, 40/Psalm 106
21	Isaiah 41, 42/Hebrews 5
22	Isaiah 43, 44/Hebrews 6
23	Isaiah 45, 46/Psalm 107
24	Isaiah 47, 48/Hebrews 7
25	Isaiah 49, 50/Hebrews 8
26	Isaiah 51, 52/Hebrews 9
27	Isaiah 53, 54/Psalms 108, 109
28	Isaiah 55, 56/Hebrews 10
29	Isaiah 57, 58/Hebrews 11
30	Isaiah 59, 60/Psalms 110, 111

the world. For instance, you may notice the warm-hearted appeal for repentance in 1:18: "Come now, let us argue it out, says the LORD: though your sins are like scarlet, they shall be like snow."

There are at least two major sections in Isaiah: chapters 1—40 and chapters 41—66. Some think that chapters 56—66 are a third division. The sections are clearly distinguishable, and they reflect such different periods in the history of the Jews that many think the latter section was written by a follower, or followers, of Isaiah. We can't sort all that out here, but it may be helpful to be aware that the first forty chapters are set in the later years of the Southern Kingdom, Judah, while the rest of the book refers to the period after the fall of the kingdom and the exile of the people to Babylon.

Isaiah is especially interesting because it contains many Messianic passages. Examples are chapters 7, 9, 11, 42, and 53. You may want to look for New Testament parallels to other passages as well—for instance, 28:16; 35:5–6; 56:7; and 61:1–2. Isaiah 7 is most fascinating, because it illustrates so clearly the tendency of Old Testament prophecy to contain a dual reference both to the present and to the future. On the one hand, this chapter relates directly to the reign of King Ahaz, who didn't believe (or didn't care) that God was with Judah. Isaiah tells Ahaz that he will receive a sign: a young woman will soon bear a son. As evidence of her faith in the midst of desperate circumstances, she will name her child "Immanuel." On the other hand, however, this prophecy of a sign for Ahaz can be broadened and deepened so that it points to the birth of another child, the Christ. He is born of a virgin and is Immanuel in the fullest sense: he himself is "God with us."

Our readings in the New Testament this month will complete the letters of Paul and take us through most of the book of Hebrews. Hebrews was written by someone who was steeped in the Jewish Scriptures. In the early days of the church, Paul's name became associated with the book, but for centuries scholars have recognized that the style of Hebrews is very different from that of Paul. Educated guesses are that Barnabas or Apollos were the authors, but there is no certainty about this.

Whoever the author was, he seems to be writing to Jewish believers in Christ who were tempted to return to Judaism, perhaps because of imminent persecution. To ward off this possibility, the author of Hebrews offers a kind of extended proof that Jesus Christ fulfills, and is superior to, all that we find in the Old Testament. You will find the reasoning complex, as the author not only plays on the meaning of individual words but also draws allegorical implications from a variety of Old Testament passages.

The heart of the book is found in the description of Jesus as the great high priest who far surpasses the priesthood of Israel (chs. 4—8). Because of Christ's ministry, a new and better covenant has been established. This covenant is eternal and final, because it is based on Christ's own sacrifice.

Notice that, from beginning to end, Hebrews stresses that all of life, and salvation as well, revolves around Jesus Christ. The writer of Hebrews thought that it was important for his readers to remember this. It is still important for us today!

In the Spotlight: September

The High Priesthood Reinterpreted

At important points in the Gospels, the texts mention "high priests," even naming two of them, Annas and Caiaphas (Luke 3:2). In fact, only one person served as high priest at any given time. Each year, the Roman governor designated a different individual to hold the post, but all of them came from the same family, rotating in and out of office. Thus, all could be spoken of collectively as "the high priests."

The high priest served as the head of the priesthood. He alone was allowed to enter the Holy of Holies in the temple annually to offer sacrifices on the Day of Atonement. Originally a religious post, the high priesthood took on broader significance following the destruction of Jerusalem and the end of the kingship. By New Testament times, the high priest functioned as the supreme Jewish authority, subject to the Romans, of course.

The book of Hebrews uses the high priesthood as an image by which to portray Jesus Christ's work of redemption. To serve as high priest, the writer explains, Jesus must be made like us "in every respect" (2:17). A priest must be able to sympathize with human weakness, which Jesus is able to do because of his own suffering (5:1–9).

The remainder of the argument goes like this: Jesus is similar to Melchizedek, the mysterious priest-king in Jerusalem to whom Abraham paid tithes (Genesis 14:20). Since Levi, the father of the tribe from which the priests descend, would be born from Abraham's family line, the Levites, too, in a sense acknowledged Melchizedek's supremacy through Abraham's tithe.

Additionally, the Levitical priesthood is limited, because it requires daily repetition of sacrifices. Jesus, however, lays down his own life as a sacrifice "once for all" (Hebrews 7:27). His priestly service never needs to be repeated. Furthermore, the Levitical priesthood is impermanent, because individual priests die and must be replaced in office by others. Since Jesus rose from the dead, however, he can serve as priest forever (7:23–25).

While you may find this extended argument difficult to follow, Jewish readers would have found it easy to understand—whether they agreed or not! By this reinterpretation, the author of Hebrews wants to illustrate the greatness of Jesus and the sufficiency of his sacrifice. The purpose, as he tells us, is to encourage us all to "approach [to God] with a true heart in full assurance of faith" (10:22).

OCTOBER

Day	Scripture Reading
1	Isaiah 61, 62/Hebrews 12
2	Isaiah 63, 64/Hebrews 13
3	Isaiah 65, 66/John 1
4	Jeremiah 1, 2/Psalms 112, 113
5	Jeremiah 3, 4/John 2
6	Jeremiah 5, 6/John 3
7	Jeremiah 7, 8/Psalms 114, 115
8	Jeremiah 9, 10/John 4
9	Jeremiah 11, 12/John 5
10	Jeremiah 13, 14/John 6
11	Jeremiah 15, 16/Psalm 116
12	Jeremiah 17, 18/John 7
13	Jeremiah 19, 20/John 8
14	Jeremiah 21, 22/Psalms 117, 118
15	Jeremiah 23, 24/John 9
16	Jeremiah 25, 26/John 10
17	Jeremiah 27, 28/John 11
18	Jeremiah 29–31/Psalm 119:1-24
19	Jeremiah 32, 33/John 12
20	Jeremiah 34, 35/John 13
21	Jeremiah 36, 37/Psalm 119:25-48
22	Jeremiah 38, 39/John 14
23	Jeremiah 40, 41/ John 15
24	Jeremiah 42, 43/John 16
25	Jeremiah 44–46/Psalm 119:49-72
26	Jeremiah 47, 48/John 17
27	Jeremiah 49, 50/John 18
28	Jeremiah 51, 52/Psalm 119:73-96
29	Lamentations 1, 2/John 19
30	Lamentations 3–5/John 20
31	Ezekiel 1/1 John 21

Most of our reading in the Old Testament this month will be in the second of the "Major Prophets," Jeremiah. The reason that these books are called "major" is simple: they are much longer than the twelve books called the "Minor Prophets."

Jeremiah was from a priestly family. We read at the beginning of the book that he felt called to his prophetic ministry at a young age. Like Moses years before him (Exodus 3—4), Jeremiah was hesitant and attempted to excuse himself from the call (1:6). Unknowingly, he had good reason to. You would consider his later life as a prophet pleasant only if you enjoy being beaten and placed in stocks (20:2), thrown into a dungeon (37:16), dropped into a muddy cistern (38:6), and threatened with death (26:11). Even the people of Jeremiah's own hometown wanted to kill him (11:21). Fortunately, Jeremiah had a trusted secretary, Baruch, who put his prophecies into writing and seems to have been a friend to him (ch. 36).

When you read Jeremiah, it will be obvious why the leaders in Judah disliked this man and his message. Jeremiah preached doom. He announced that Jerusalem, including the temple itself, would be destroyed. The reason he gave for this prophecy was the faithlessness of the people. Jeremiah proclaimed that their injustice, unrighteousness, and disbelief had reached such a point that God's only recourse was to execute judgment.

As with most of the prophetic books, you will want to read quickly, looking for the main theme rather than puzzling over the details of each verse or paragraph. The book of Jeremiah is not written in a strictly chronological order, and that can make the details seem even more confusing. Try to gain an appreciation for Jeremiah's personality and to observe his anguish at the self-destructive behavior of his people. He truly grieves as he watches his people deny the God they profess to worship by the way they live their lives.

Still, Jeremiah offers more than relentless doom and gloom. The core of his message includes a deeply cherished hope. You will find this hope in chapters 31—32, where Jeremiah foresees a new covenant. This may remind you of the book of Hebrews, which we read last month. Hebrews points out that the forgiveness and inward renewal of the heart prophesied by Jeremiah are offered to us through the great high priest, Jesus Christ (Hebrews 8—9).

This month most of the readings from the New Testament will come from John. It is a favorite book for many people, even though it can seem a bit wordy and repetitious at times. That is because the book looks at Christ from different angles. John is written in a simple style with an easy vocabulary. (For that reason, it is often chosen as the book to read in teaching Greek to seminary students.) However, the external simplicity is deceiving. John's descriptions of the Christ are exceptionally profound, and you can read them repeatedly without ever uncovering all the depths and riches they contain.

The contrast between John and the other three Gospels is startling. The Synoptic Gospels, as they are called, provide us with an overview of the life of Jesus, and they give us some detail about a host of incidents in his life. John, by comparison, is not very concerned about extensive descriptions of the events in Jesus' life. Rather, he wants us to focus on the meaning, or inner side, of the events. He wants us to get below the surface of things to see their significance.

A sign of this is John's tendency to hint at two levels of meaning in what he says. For example, notice the comment that Nicodemus comes to Jesus "by night" (3:2). On one level, this indicates Nicodemus's concern to avoid being seen with Jesus. However, when you recall John's contrast of light with darkness (1:5), it is obvious that there is another level here. Nicodemus does not know the light; he is still "in the dark" regarding the One who is the true "light of the world" (8:12).

This is the meaning of the "signs" in John. Beginning with the transformation of water to wine at Cana in chapter 2, and concluding with the raising of Lazarus in chapter 11, Jesus performs seven marvelous actions. On one level, each of these is a miraculous physical event accomplished by Jesus, but John uses each of them to delineate something deeper and much more profound about the identity of Jesus and the meaning of salvation and eternal life. Can you find all seven signs? What do you think is the deeper significance of each?

There is no doubt about John's ultimate goal in all of this. At the beginning of the book, he tells us that Jesus Christ is the Word, or Son, of God. Jesus is true God come in the flesh. Near the end of the book, even the doubting disciple himself, Thomas, affirms this same conclusion: "My Lord and my God!" (20:28). Then John tells us explicitly that he has written all of this "that you may come to believe that Jesus is the Messiah, the Son of God, and that through believing you may have life in his name" (v. 31).

In the Spotlight: October

Jeremiah and the Prophets of Israel

Jeremiah illustrates a number of characteristics that are found in one or another of Israel's prophets. While there were families of prophets in Israel, most of the prophets whose names we know seem to have come from diverse walks of life. Jeremiah came from a priestly family. Amos was a shepherd. Some, like Amos, appear on the scene briefly, while others, like Jeremiah and Isaiah, played a part in Jerusalem's history for a number of decades.

The prophets receive their messages in various ways. Some see visions; others dream dreams; still others hear voices. Some may simply have reflected on the events of the day and felt compelled to deliver a "word from the Lord."

There were obviously many prophets in Israel, as frequent denunciations of "false prophets" make clear. The fact that prophets could announce words from the Lord that contradicted each other undoubtedly made it difficult for people to know whom to believe. Occasionally, the text identifies a false prophet by name, but usually we learn little about him. Nor do we get much sense of the lives of the prophets whose names we do know. The anecdotes about Jeremiah are an exception.

All of the prophets seem to have sensed a special call from God. Again, as with Jeremiah, we sometimes read a story of their call. Note Isaiah 6, Ezekiel 1, and Amos 7. Sometimes the prophets are reluctant to accept that call, but they are unable to avoid it for long. Shortly, they find themselves speaking as messengers of Israel's God: "Thus says the Lord."

Oftentimes, the prophets declare that the power of their message is because "the Spirit of the Lord" is on them. Usually, unfortunately, the messages they bring are ones the rulers, or the people, do not want to hear. Some of the prophets, like Jeremiah, suffer for their proclamations.

If we ask why their messages are resisted, the answer is easy. The prophets insist that Israel's faith and behavior must be rooted in central themes of liberation from Egypt and the covenant at Mt. Sinai: freedom from bondage, the call to righteous living, and the demand for justice for all. In the life of the people of the later Northern and Southern Kingdoms, these principles were frequently subverted. The prophets, however, could not remain silent, and so they pronounced their frequently unwelcome "words from the Lord."

NOVEMBER

This month we will cover a good deal of ground in our year with the Bible. The New Testament readings include a number of small books called the "general epistles." Although they are written by different authors and are addressed to people in divergent situations, they should be relatively familiar and easy to follow. That's good, because the Old Testament readings may make you feel as if you are going around in circles (to borrow an image from Ezekiel 1).

In the Old Testament, we will be reading Ezekiel and Daniel. Ezekiel is a curious figure whose tendency to speak in symbolic language makes his prophetic work seem especially strange and complicated. He lived through the most devastating event in Israel's history: the conquest of Jerusalem by the Babylonian Empire in 587 B.C. He himself had already been taken to Babylon with an earlier group of exiles, and, in the years just preceding the calamity, he was called to prophesy impending doom. Remember that many voices were claiming that God would never permit the holy city to undergo serious harm. Ezekiel, however, now joined his older compatriot, Jeremiah, in announcing that divine judgment was both imminent and inevitable.

Day	Scripture Reading	
1	Ezekiel 2, 3/Psalms 119:97–120	•
2	Ezekiel 4, 5/James 1	▸
3	Ezekiel 6, 7/James 2	⸱
4	Ezekiel 8, 9/Psalm 119:121–144	▸
5	Ezekiel 10, 11/James 3	◢
6	Ezekiel 12, 13/James 4	◂
7	Ezekiel 14, 15/James 5	⸱
8	Ezekiel 16, 17/ Psalm 119:145–176	•
9	Ezekiel 18, 19/1 Peter 1	•
10	Ezekiel 20, 21/1 Peter 2	◥
11	Ezekiel 22, 23/Psalms 120–122	◂
12	Ezekiel 24, 25/1 Peter 3	⸱
13	Ezekiel 26, 27/1 Peter 4	•
14	Ezekiel 28, 29/1 Peter 5	◀
15	Ezekiel 30, 31/Psalms 123–125	▾
16	Ezekiel 32, 33/2 Peter 1	◂
17	Ezekiel 34, 35/2 Peter 2	◂
18	Ezekiel 36, 37/Psalms 126–128	⸱
19	Ezekiel 38, 39/2 Peter 3	◀
20	Ezekiel 40, 41/1 John 1	◀
21	Ezekiel 42, 43/1 John 2	⸱
22	Ezekiel 44, 45/Psalms 129–131	◥
23	Ezekiel 46, 47/1 John 3	⸱
24	Ezekiel 48/1 John 4	◂
25	Daniel 1–3/Psalms 132–134	◂
26	Daniel 4, 5/1 John 5	◥
27	Daniel 6, 7/2 John 1	◉
28	Daniel 8, 9/3 John 1	⸱
29	Daniel 10–12/Psalms 135, 136	◂
30	Hosea 1, 2/Jude	◀

Chapter 1 gives us the record of Ezekiel's call in highly visionary language. If you are thirty or younger, you'll be happy to know that the rabbis found this vision to be so intricate and complex that they felt it should be studied only by those over the age of thirty. (So you won't be disappointed, however, we will allow you to read it this year!) The basic imagery conveys the ideas of divine judgment (a storm out of the north), the omnipresence and omniscience of an almighty God (wheels, eyes, and likenesses of animals), and the majesty of a mysterious yet merciful God (the throne, the human form, and the rainbow).

As with earlier prophetic books, you will want to read Ezekiel quickly. Keep in mind that the first twenty-four chapters offer prophecies related to the coming judgment on Jerusalem. Then Ezekiel prophesies doom to a number of other nations (chapters 25—32). Finally, the remainder of the book speaks about future restoration for God's people, climaxing in chapters 40—48 with a highly symbolic portrait of a renewed temple.

Look, too, for images and symbols in Ezekiel that are important in the New Testament: the vine, the good shepherd, the new heart, the indwelling Spirit, an everlasting covenant, the river of life, and a new Jerusalem. If you search for it, you will find an amazing wealth of spiritual insight in Ezekiel.

Like Ezekiel, Daniel is an interesting book. You may remember the stories of Daniel and his friends from your childhood. The rest of the book, though, with its enigmatic imagery and psychedelic visions, might keep you awake at night! Actually, it should do the opposite because the primary message of the visions is that God is sovereign. We can rest secure in the knowledge that the Lord controls the world. Kings and rulers are subject to God's irresistible will, and the course of history is in God's hand.

We cannot go into the controversies here about the dating of this book, but you should be aware that there are sharp disagreements among those who feel that the entire book was compiled at about the time of the Babylonian Captivity, late in the sixth century B.C., and those who believe that much of it was put together at about the middle of the second century B.C.

In any case, notice that the visionary material is very different from most of what we have read in the prophetic books, and it has come to be called "apocalyptic" (which means "revelation"). It is quite similar to what we will read in the New Testament book of Revelation next month. Bear in mind that the goal of this kind of writing is to assure readers that they can and should trust in God, in spite of how bleak or disheartening the difficulties and trials they face may appear to be.

The material in the New Testament is much easier to follow. James, 1 Peter, and 1 John are the most significant of the seven letters we will be reading. As you will observe, the letters differ markedly in style and tone, and they emphasize different themes. All of the letters intend to bolster the faith of their readers and encourage them to live exemplary Christian lives. Some of them suggest a rather rigorous tone, which may lead us to ask whether we, in the present, really take our Christian discipleship seriously enough. What would any of these writers say if they were speaking to our congregation today?

Look for passages that stress God's faithfulness, both in the present and in the future. It is hard for us today, in our situation of relative ease and comfort, to recognize how much pressure early Christians felt under the ever-present threat of persecution. That is why they needed to be reminded so strongly of God's abiding faithfulness. That is also why they needed to hear the kind of benediction that we read at the end of Jude, one that is good for us to hear as well: "Now to him who is able to keep you from falling . . . , to the only God our Savior, through Jesus Christ our Lord, be glory, majesty, power, and authority, before all time and now and forever. Amen" (vv. 24–25).

In the Spotlight: November

The Epistle of James

When Martin Luther translated the New Testament into German at the time of the Reformation, he concluded that the epistle of James did not match the quality of the apostle Paul's letters and theology. Luther called the letter "an epistle of straw" and placed it at the end of his translation. His dislike made most Protestant churches suspicious of the epistle. James has always been better received in the Roman Catholic and Eastern Orthodox Churches, and it is only in recent decades that Protestants, too, have come to appreciate the writing.

The epistle is attributed to James, the brother of Jesus. James, along with the other brothers, does not seem to have believed in Jesus until after the resurrection (John 7:5; Acts 1:14). Paul tells us that, among Jesus' resurrection appearances, he manifested himself individually to James (1 Corinthians 15:7). Later James became the acknowledged head of the church at Jerusalem (Acts 15:13), until he was martyred around A.D. 62. In later tradition, James was revered for his singular piety and holy life.

Scholars debate whether James is the author of this epistle. The high quality of the Greek makes it unlikely that he wrote it as it stands. Because of the Jewish character of the epistle, however, and because of its similarities to Jesus' own words and thought pattern in the Synoptic Gospels, some scholars hold that an unknown writer pulled together sermons and other materials from James and edited them into this form, which is more of a homily than an epistle.

The most famous section of James is the discussion in chapter 2 about faith and works to which Luther objected so strenuously. However, the text is not talking about whether faith or works is the basis for salvation, but rather whether or not our treatment of others corresponds with the faith we claim to possess. Note the humorous—and sarcastic—question about what profit there is for people who are poor or starving if you wish them God's peace but then simply walk away (2:14–17).

The importance of living a consistent, compassionate, and moral life is a central theme throughout the letter. Other themes include the need for wisdom, the importance of steadfastness, the significance of humility, and the dangers of uncontrolled speech. Underlying the whole is the sense that to practice all of these virtues faithfully we will need to be sustained by a continuous and serious life of prayer.

DECEMBER

Day	Scripture Reading	
1	Hosea 3–6/Revelation 1	
2	Hosea 7, 8/Psalms 137, 138	
3	Hosea 9, 10/Revelation 2	
4	Hosea 11, 12/Revelation 3	
5	Hosea 13, 14/Revelation 4	
6	Joel 1, 2/Psalm 139	
7	Joel 3/Revelation 5	
8	Amos 1, 2/Revelation 6	
9	Amos 3, 4/Psalms 140, 141	
10	Amos 5, 6/Revelation 7	
11	Amos 7, 8/Revelation 8	
12	Amos 9/Revelation 9	
13	Obadiah 1/Psalms 142, 143	
14	Jonah 1, 2/Revelation 10	
15	Jonah 3, 4/Revelation 11	
16	Micah 1–3/Psalm 144	
17	Micah 4, 5/Revelation 12	
18	Micah 6, 7/Revelation 13	
19	Nahum 1–3/Revelation 14	
20	Habakkuk 1–3/Psalm 145	
21	Zephaniah 1–3/Revelation 15	
22	Haggai 1, 2/Revelation 16	
23	Zechariah 1, 2/Psalms 146, 147	
24	Zechariah 3, 4/Revelation 17	
25	Zechariah 5, 6/Revelation 18	
26	Zechariah 7, 8/Revelation 19	
27	Zechariah 9, 10/Psalm 148	
28	Zechariah 11, 12/Revelation 20	
29	Zechariah 13, 14/Revelation 21	
30	Malachi 1, 2/Psalms 149, 150	
31	Malachi 3, 4/Revelation 22	

Here we are! These are the last month's readings in *The Year of the Bible*. Let's hope that we are still on target, or at least positioned to make a run for the goal in December. In this last month, we will be reading the Minor Prophets of the Old Testament and one very curious book in the New Testament, the book of Revelation.

As you may know, the primary reason that the last twelve books of the Old Testament are called the "Minor Prophets" is that they are generally quite brief—certainly in comparison to Isaiah, Jeremiah, and Ezekiel. They were written at different times and places. Some of the books tell us where and when they were written, but others do not. Unless you have extra time to spare, it is not wise to try to puzzle out the historical background. You will be better off simply reading the books and looking for main themes and familiar passages.

The basic themes of the Minor Prophets are similar to those in the other books of the prophets: God's judgment on sin and disobedience; the call to repentance and righteous living; the assurance of continuing mercy and forgiveness after judgment; and the promise of a Last Day that will bring final judgment and a blessed new world of peace and love. You will not find these themes neatly organized in the books, nor will you find all of the themes in all of the books. If you keep these themes in mind, however, you will have a better idea of the overall picture in God's message through these prophets.

Here are some brief comments about a few of the Minor Prophets. Hosea demonstrates the continuing mercy and faithfulness of God through his own steadfast commitment to a faithless wife, Gomer. If you have ever thought of God as cold and distant, look at the warmth and compassion that are evident here in God's longing for this errant people. Amos reminds Israel of something that Samuel had told Saul many years earlier: Religious practices (worship, offerings, and the like) do not please God unless they are coupled with an upright, good life (5:21–24; see 1 Samuel 15:22).

Micah makes this same point, using words that may sound familiar, when he says that what the Lord requires of us is "to do justice, and to love kindness, and to walk humbly with your God" (6:8). There is another familiar verse in Micah that you have probably heard many times. You will undoubtedly hear it quoted again this month. Look at 5:2 to see what it is.

Habakkuk almost loses his faith because of the evil and unrighteousness that he experiences, but at the end of the book he concludes with a ringing affirmation of faith and trust in the Lord—even if he should lose everything (3:17–18). Remember this passage during those times when you encounter grief and loss in your own life.

Our readings in the New Testament this month will be in the book of Revelation. Revelation has caused more confusion and consternation than any other book in the Bible. Seemingly, there are as many interpretations as there are students of the book. Many people believe that, if we read Revelation carefully enough, we can determine the time of the end of the world. Or, even if we cannot arrive at the precise time of the end, we can at least pin down the generation that will see the end come. However, this is not a very profitable way to approach Revelation. Many people through the centuries have tried to predict the time of the end—and failed!

It is more profitable to look at the many symbols in Revelation in terms of how they give us a glimpse of the glory of God and Christ. Notice the awe-inspiring vision of Jesus Christ right at the beginning of the book (1:12–20). The wealth of images and allusions here shows us just how powerful symbolic, poetic language can be. It portrays in an especially compelling manner the authority, majesty, and might of the risen and exalted Christ.

Poetic portraits like this, not only of Christ but also of God, are scattered throughout the book. Another example is the vision in chapter 4, where John sees heaven opened and God (who is not described) seated on a throne. The various elements of this royal court serve to show us how great and magnificent the Lord of heaven and earth really is: "You are worthy, our Lord and God, to receive glory and honor and power" (4:11).

One major thing to look for in Revelation: how the book brings home to us the final victory of God over the forces of evil in the universe. That is really what all those fantastic descriptions of cataclysmic events contained in the seven seals, the seven trumpets, and the seven bowls mean to tell us. It does not matter how frightening the beasts, the dragons, the armies of Satan, or even Satan himself, seem to be. God is in control, and world history will unfold according to a firm divine plan. In God's own time and way, the Lord will wreak havoc on all of the forces of sin, evil, and unrighteousness.

The final two chapters of Revelation, with their vision of a new heaven and a new earth, conclude our readings in *The Year of the Bible*. Read these chapters slowly; meditate on them. They picture our ultimate hope of a new age in which God will dwell with us in a renewed world where sin and sorrow, pain and death, are no more, and where life is full and good and blessed. John finds this vision so tantalizing that he exclaims at the end, "Amen. Come, Lord Jesus!" (v. 20). May this vision also tantalize us and sustain us as we live in this world and seek to serve our Lord. Oh, yes, one more thing. Don't stop reading your Bible just because *The Year of the Bible* has ended!

In the Spotlight: December

Revelation and Apocalyptic Literature

The book of Revelation has often been interpreted as prophecy. It appears to predict the end of the world, and it has been used frequently to calculate the date of this earth-shattering event. The book belongs to a genre of literature that had become popular over the previous three centuries. Called *apocalyptic,* meaning "revelatory," such literature painted graphic images of warfare between the armies of God and the devil, described the great horrors that would accompany these struggles, and promised victory and final salvation to those who were righteous and persevered in their faith in God.

Apocalyptic literature seems to have flourished at difficult periods in Israel's history, such as the Babylonian exile, or during Hellenistic rule over Israel in the second century B.C., leading up to the Maccabean Revolt. At such times, the overwhelming power of hostile regimes made restoration for Israel seem hopeless. Apocalyptic writers found a solution by depicting Israel's God as intervening radically to establish a new world. The "age to come" would provide the justice, security, and blessings for the righteous that were lacking in this age.

In the Old Testament, sections of some of the prophets are written in the apocalyptic style. Ezekiel, Joel, Zechariah, and especially the second half of Daniel provide good examples. The same style can be found in materials that are not part of the Old Testament, such as the book called 1 Enoch and some of the writings from the Dead Sea Scrolls.

In the New Testament, bits and pieces of this style can be found in the Gospels and in the letters of Paul, but the book of Revelation itself is the primary instance of apocalyptic literature. Increasing repression of the church in the Roman Empire, climaxing in the outright persecution by the emperor Domitian in the mid-90s, set the stage for the book. The author employs symbols such as the dragon and the beast to depict the Roman rulers as agents of Satan, and the strange, enigmatic symbols of scrolls, bowls, and trumpets predict vividly God's judgments on the power of evil.

Like apocalyptic literature in general, Revelation wants those who are oppressed for their faith to know that, despite appearances, God is sovereign; evil will be defeated in the end; and it is therefore worthwhile for believers to persevere and trust in the Lord. A new heaven and earth await them at the end.